6·50

D0994198

**THE UNIVERSITY
OF BIRMINGHAM**

INFORMATION SER

WANDERING

Common Problems with the Elderly Confused

WANDERING

Graham Stokes
BA, MSc, PhD, ABPsS

Series Editor: Una P Holden

WINSLOW PRESS
Telford Road, Bicester, Oxon OX6 0TS
Telephone: Bicester (0869) 244644

First published in 1986 by
Winslow Press, Telford Road, Bicester, Oxon OX6 0TS
Reprinted 1988
© Graham Stokes, 1988

ISBN 0 86388 042 8

1664628

02–150 Printed in Great Britain by Hobbs the Printers, Southampton

CONTENTS

Dr Graham Stokes is a senior clinical psychologist at Walsgrave Hospital, Coventry, with special responsibility for psychology services to the elderly. He graduated from the University of Leeds in 1976 and obtained his doctorate and qualification in clinical psychology at the University of Birmingham. Since qualifying he has worked in the field of adult mental health and now specialises in the psychological management of the confused elderly.

SECTION 1
Discovery

1

The Strain of Managing the Elderly Wanderer

Caring for an elderly confused person can be dificult at the best of times as they slowly lose touch with reality and become less able to carry out basic everyday tasks. However, when that person becomes disturbed and disruptive, providing sympathetic care can seem an impossible goal. One of the most demanding behaviours to cope with is that of persistent and often seeminly meaningless WANDERING.

Wandering is a common behaviour among the confused elderly, and is in part the result of deteriorating memory and declining capacity to think and reason. This not only affects their ability to explain and communicate the purpose of wandering, but makes it increasingly likely that wanderers will be unable to remember the reason why they decided to move about. However, wandering is not always closely linked to the severity of memory loss or intellectual deterioration. Even those people who are only mildly confused and are reasonably independent may wander and become lost or disturb neighbours.

Family Care

Owing to the nature of the problem, wandering is difficult for supporters to manage and because of the risk of serious falls, road traffic accidents and exposure to extreme weather, can have serious consequences for the wanderer. Wandering can occur during day or night; the family of a wanderer living at home will have little peace of mind or time for rest. The unexpected disappearance from home of an elderly person, unsuitably dressed, can cause the carer great worry and lead to constant nagging doubts about security and safety. This heavy burden of responsibility together with the draining effect of broken nights as the wanderer roams around the house can be an intolerable source of stress. Feelings of apprehension, embarrassment, helplessness, anger and resentment are common. Distress over a spouse or parent who becomes odd, absent-minded or muddled is normal and understandable. However, the excessive stress and strain of managing a person who wanders can tax resources to the limit and may be responsible for an upsetting breakdown in the ability of a husband or wife, son or daughter to care for their confused loved one at home. Time after time families report that the need to provide constant supervision, especially if the problem is one of wandering at night, can make life unbearable.

Residential Care

Around half the residents of ordinary residential homes are handicapped by dementia, and so the strain of caring affects not only relatives struggling to cope with the problem at home, but can also lead to feelings of frustration and despair among care staff. Pleading with a wanderer to sit down, stop irritating other residents and to stay away from exits can fall on seemingly deaf ears. Efforts to entice the elderly wanderer to join in activities invariably flounder in the face of their determination to keep on the move. Concern for the wanderers' welfare can become acute as a watchful eye cannot always be guaranteed — especially when there are staff shortages. Moreover, it is wrong of those who wish to protect the wanderer from danger to assume that most residential homes and hospitals are designed to cater for the safety of those who are frequently wandering and becoming lost. They are not. For these reasons, staff may become anxious about their responsibility to protect residents or patients and as a result, restricting the movement of the wanderer may seem the only solution. However, if this means locking doors and restricting access to areas within the home this can lead to additional concern that 'innocent' residents are being deprived of freedom and movement. Such action unfortunately may confirm the negative image many people have of institutional care.

When faced with these management difficulties the need for specialist skills to cope with the problem of wandering is crucial. The more a carer understands about the reasons for this behaviour the better equipped he or she will be to manage the situation effectively, and the more likely to be able to prevent difficulties arising. Unfortunately a common impression is that once memory loss occurs there is little that can be done to change the confused person's behaviour. Whilst no 'cure' exists, this pessimistic attitude is unwarranted.

Behaviour *can* be changed and it is the purpose of this book to give practical help to nurses, care staff and relatives on handling some of the difficult situations which arise when confronting the problem of wandering. There are no magic answers, nor foolproof interventions, but there is plenty of evidence to show that considerable improvement is possible.

Keyword Summary

Wandering
- A common problem

Family care
- The risk of accidents
- Feelings of worry and anger

Residential care
- Despair among care staff
- The strain of keeping a watchful eye

Specialist skills
- The need for understanding
- Improvement is possible
- Practical help for nurses, care staff and relatives

Why is it Happening?

In the same way as it is wrong to assume that all old people are alike simply because they are elderly, it is also a mistake to think that all those who wander are doing it for exactly the same reasons and therefore will raise identical management problems. There are many different reasons why an elderly confused person may start to wander, and each type of wandering behaviour will require a different response from staff or relatives.

The starting point must be – Is this person wandering?

Definition

Wandering is a tendency to keep on the move, either in an aimless or confused fashion, or in pursuit of an indefinable or unobtainable goal.

From this definition it is clearly not always the case that any elderly confused person who walks around the home or appears unaccompanied in the street is wandering. Nevertheless, because they cannot provide a well-argued reason for their presence, as an alert and competent elderly person would more easily do, these people are often labelled as wanderers and whisked back to where they came from in order that a protective eye can be kept on them. So, remember, not every absent-minded or muddled old person who is out and about is necessarily wandering. They may simply be taking a harmless stroll or enjoying a simple pleasure!

However, once you have identified the existence of a genuine problem, it is important to understand why it is occurring, bearing in mind that the confused are unlikely to know or to be able to recall why they are wandering.

Possible Explanations

Separation-anxiety

Because of their poor memory for recent events (known as short-term memory loss), an elderly person may wander because they have no recollection of how long a carer has been gone, where they have gone to, or any message to the effect that the caring relative will soon return. Wandering occurs as efforts are made to locate the reassuring presence of the carer. Even if the reason for this behaviour is forgotten the feelings of insecurity and agitation will maintain it.

Searching

An attempt to find something which is or somebody who is unobtainable. Seeking a deceased loved one, usually a parent or a spouse, is common. On occasions, a person may no longer recognise the home in which they live as their own and may insist on leaving. Many confused wanderers are 'stalkers of old haunts' as they try to seek out a world they remember, but which is likely to be long gone. They are often men who once had a routine of going out to work, walking the dog or going to the local pub. Despite becoming forgetful and confused, the habit of going out remains, although the ability to successfully make the visit and return safely has become increasingly suspect. The saying 'old habits die hard' can be only too true!

Boredom

Many confused old people lack exercise and interest and so could be wandering out of sheer boredom. The behaviour may be accompanied by gestures as if cleaning or performing work. This restless activity seeking is also more common in men. If the confused person has been used to a high level of activity, the tendency to wander can put carers under extreme pressure.

Loneliness

The confused old person who lives alone may be wandering because of loneliness. However, loneliness cannot be remedied simply by the company of just anybody. So wandering can also occur even in residential settings where other people may be seen as strangers. The problem is more common in those who have lost a spouse.

Physical discomfort

As walking can ease discomfort, a confused person who is in pain due to earache, toothache or constipation, for example, may start wandering. Sitting down with little to distract the mind from the sensation of pain can only lead to an increased awareness of the distressing ailment.

Coping with stress

If a person used to obtain relief from stress through taking a brisk walk or a long stroll, then wandering can be a confused continuation of this life-long pattern of coping. A change in routine or living arrangements could therefore be responsible for an episode of agitated wandering.

Apparently aimless wandering

A person may get up with a task or plan in mind, but then forget what they had intended to do, leaving them wandering aimlessly with no obvious motive. On occasions, a knowledge that there was a reason which can no longer be recalled can result in the person wandering around the home becoming increasingly agitated, muttering about having to do, or find, this or that, in a confused attempt to gain peace of mind.

Disorientation

Wandering can occur following arrival at a new placement. A person who is unfamiliar with their surroundings may roam around the building searching for the toilet, dining room, etc, innocently entering the rooms of other residents and causing aggravation and upset. Such wandering can lead to further troublesome problems such as inappropriate urinating, repetitive questioning and aggressive incidents. Even when a person has lived for many years in the same house they can become disorientated as their confusion worsens.

Night-time wandering

Confused wandering can be most marked at night. This is not usually the result of fatigue. The hours of darkness and silence can easily disorientate the elderly with memory loss as they rely on information from the environment to keep in touch with reality. So a confused person with no history of wandering, may start roaming about at night after moving to a residential home in an effort to seek clues as to their whereabouts. Whilst this is likely to be only a temporary difficulty during the settling-in period, there is always the constant problem of sensory deprivation at night, for darkness also makes it easier to misinterpret shapes, shadows and unexpected noises. For example, shadows may resemble a prowler, a lampstand may resemble a person standing by the bed. When this leads to wandering, the wanderer is likely to be agitated and frightened.

Another problem is that many elderly people suffer from various forms of insomnia. This can result in their becoming restless and therefore wandering around the home or ward at night with an inappropriate objective in mind, eg wanting to go out, wishing to have a meal, etc. However, we must also bear in mind that old people do not require much more than 5 or 6 hours' sleep at night.

Attention-seeking

By creating disruption and difficulties a person who is receiving less attention than usual or an amount insufficient for their needs can force carers to take more notice of them and give them more of their time. Because of its implications, wandering can be a powerful means of gaining attention.

So, as you can see, wandering is by no means a straightforward problem either to understand or resolve.

Keyword Summary

Wandering
- A definition
- Is the person wandering?

Possible explanations
- Separation anxiety
- Searching
- Boredom
- Loneliness
- Physical discomfort
- Coping with stress
- Apparently aimless wandering
- Disorientation
- Night-time wandering
- Attention-seeking

◆3◆

Making Matters Worse

Whilst changes in memory and intellect contribute to the problem of wandering, when seeking a more complete explanation we must clearly take into account environmental influences and appreciate the extra problems that inadequate living arrangements, poor quality of life and inappropriate management procedures can bring about.

Residential Settings

In some homes for the elderly, inactivity is the norm. Bored residents spend most of the day sitting or lying down doing nothing, with only mealtimes to look forward to.

Having plenty of time to do so little is made worse by feelings of being alone. Despite living with other people, an elderly resident has on average as little as eight minutes conversation each hour. This is usually with other residents, for staff normally spend time with residents only when they are 'doing' something for them. Unfortunately, those residents who are the most confused tend to be even less involved and are more likely to be ignored. That is, until they start to become difficult or disruptive. Giving excessive attention to a person who wanders, even if it is borne out of a wish to protect or care for the wanderer, can lead to an unwanted increase in this behaviour, especially if this is the only time a fuss is made of the person. Some old people are flattered by the responses of carers and others (eg policemen) to wandering, although some may become distressed or agitated if the approach is one of confrontation and excitement.

Depriving elderly people of cherished possessions which offer continuity with the past and reassurance can rouse a feeling of distressing insecurity. Without personal momentoes to help someone reminisce about their experiences and achievements, memories of the past fade and seen unreal. Such an unpleasant break with personal history can easily make elderly confused residents feel they do not belong in their new surroundings.

Even the physical design of a home and the care regime adopted by staff can aggravate the situation. Unpredictable washing, dressing and toileting routines, variable mealtimes, inadequate lighting (especially at night), frequent staff changes, absence of clocks, uniform colour schemes and a lack of information which make it difficult for residents to find their way from one location to another, are just some of the features of residential life which have to be considered when seeking the reasons for disoriented behaviour.

Night-time routines can also increase the problem of wandering. Often the many hours old people spend in bed at a stretch are for the convenience of staff not residents. Sticking rigidly to a routine can mean residents being put to bed at the same time night after night, regardless of whether they are tired or what their pre-sleeping habits had been before they entered the home. The outcome can be restless nights and nocturnal wandering. These difficulties are even more likely to arise when inactivity results in residents cat-napping during the day.

Physical Handicaps

A large number of old people suffer from poor hearing and eyesight, yet these handicaps are often left unattended (as are many minor ailments and illnesses which cause discomfort and irritation), and, unwisely, are not considered relevant when considering why a person may be wandering.

Trying to Find a Solution

Whilst all these conditions make wandering more likely to occur, the reaction to the problem can lead to further difficulties and an accelerated 'deterioration' in the confused person's behaviour. It is often the case that when wandering becomes increasingly difficult to manage, a change in routine or placement takes place. Attendance at a day centre may be arranged, relatives may need a period of rest and so respite care in a hospital or residential home may be requested. Alternatively, a confused person may start to disrupt a lounge of quiet residents and be moved to another unit. Whilst the reasons for these actions are understandable, because a failing memory makes it difficult for the elderly confused to adjust to strange and often unhelpful environments, frequent changes serve to increase disorientation, stress and thus also the likelihood of wandering.
 Unfortunately, the response of some care staff who may have little knowledge of the problem and

are often working under pressure can do more harm than good. An example is when members of staff employ different ideas at the same time to prevent or contain wandering. This not only causes misunderstanding, but can also increase the elderly person's confusion. Besides inconsistent work practices, other instances of unhelpful staff decisions include the inappropriate use of medication, which can easily turn a fit, if confused, old person into a drowsy and withdrawn one, and the introduction of physical restraints which can become objects of hostility and destroy the relationship between carer and wanderer. The unwise use of these methods not only intensifies and complicates the original problem, but can also obscure the true causes of wandering.

Living at Home

Finally, while it is easy to see how the conditions for wandering can unintentionally arise in a residential setting, when an old person lives at home their circumstances can promote wandering to an even greater extent. Spending hours at a time with little to do, possibly alone and feeling neglected or abandoned, can only serve to encourage disruptive behaviour such as wandering. Living in houses not designed for infirm old people – where the toilet may be far from the bedroom, possibly downstairs or outside, and where all doors look the same from the inside, including the front door – can easily increase the potential for disorientation, wandering and the risk of accidents.

Possibly the most unhelpful living arrangement is when the confused wanderer lives alone. Little contact with other people to provide a tie with reality means that the confused person can become so disorientated that day and night are reversed and the elderly wanderer may roam around the neighbourhood seeking reassurance, information, or even making absurd complaints. Unfortunately, living alone in a house full of memories can also lead to wandering. The elderly confused person may regularly live in the past and try to search for their young children, attempt to find their spouse whose return from work they are awaiting or adopt old routines such as going out to the local shops. In many ways the problems which promote wandering in the home often appear to be the most difficult to resolve as they are part and parcel of the decision to live in the community.

You can probably think of many other ways in which wandering can be unintentionally encouraged and management made more arduous.

Keyword Summary

Residential settings – environmental influences
- Inactivity
- Loneliness
- Giving excessive attention to 'disruptive' behaviour
- Loss of personal possessions and mementos
- Unhelpful surroundings and inadequate building design
- Care regimes and routines
- Special problems at night

Personal handicaps
- Poor hearing and eyesight
- Minor ailments left unattended

The response of carers
- Frequent changes of placement
- Inconsistent work practices – different staff with different ideas
- The inappropriate use of medication – tranquillizers do not solve the problem
- The use of physical constraints – targets of hostility

Living at home
- Isolation – boredom and loneliness
- Inadequate facilities
- Living alone – few ties with reality

4

Understanding the Individual Problem

Before tackling the problem of wandering, it is important to recognise that while the nature of wandering can be described in general terms (eg nocturnal, attention-seeking, aimless, searching), it has ultimately to be seen as an example of disruptive behaviour *unique* to an *individual*. We therefore need to have a thorough understanding of the elderly person's wandering as it is occurring *now*. Do not rely on guesswork or on an opinion based on a previous episode of wandering as this problem can occur in the same person at different times for different reasons.

What is Causing the Behaviour?

Wandering is not a continuous activity. Even the most active wanderer roams only about half the time. On average, wandering takes up about a third of the waking time of the person who is labelled a 'wanderer'. In order to understand why wandering is not an all-consuming behaviour, taking place at all times, we need to look at the situations in which it occurs. This involves not only identifying when wandering takes place, but also noting what the person was doing before they started to wander and what was the response of carers to the incident. This task can be easily carried out by following the **ABC analysis of behaviour**.

A = Activating event or situation
B = Behaviour (in this case wandering)
C = Consequences

Examples of questions which need to be answered under these headings are:

A
- When and where did the wandering start?
- What was the person doing immediately before they started to wander?
- What was happening around them at the time?

B
- What form did the wandering take?
- Was the person agitated, distressed or happy whilst wandering?
- Did they appear to be searching?
- Did they roam about the building or did they attempt to go outside?
- Were they talking while wandering?

C
- What was the response of carers to the wandering?
- Was the person told off; ignored; restrained; sedated; or guided back to where they had started from?

The ABCs are recorded each time an incident of wandering occurs and all staff should be aware that the behaviour is being observed. It is best to record the information at the time of the incident as it is easy to forget the exact circumstances if the recording is left until later.

As you can see, a Behavioural Analysis provides an accurate and detailed description of actual behaviour in terms of how often it occurred, the circumstances in which it arose and the consequences for the elderly wanderer. However, to complete the analysis two further areas of information need to be obtained.

Background

First, it is helpful to record the background to the wandering. For example, has anything happened during the day (or night) which may have caused upset, annoyance or excitement? Has anything out of the ordinary happened? Is the wanderer on any medication? Has there been a recent change in medication? Have there been recent changes in eating, drinking or toileting habits? Does the wanderer appear ill or in pain? Does the person suffer from poor hearing or vision? Has there been a recent bereavement?

Life History

Secondly, we must also take into account a person's life history. Was the person who wanders at night a night-shift worker? Alternatively, are they being denied the bedtime rituals and sleeping habits they observed at home? Is the person who lives alone after years of company wandering to seek companionship? Or conversely, is an elderly person who previously enjoyed a solitary existence and who starts to wander following admission to a residential home finding living with others in a confined space distressing?

The message for professional carers must be 'know your clients', otherwise the tendency to wander may be influenced by factors we may be unaware of. In order to obtain a complete personal history – eg previous lifestyle and work roles, habits at home and work, patterns of physical exercise, beliefs and expectations, sources of stress, methods of coping with change and stress, illnesses, etc – not only do care staff and other professionals need to be involved in the process, but so also does the family of the confused wanderer.

Recording the Information

The collection of all this information on possible contributory factors can be displayed on a record chart similar to the one illustrated below (with a covering sheet to provide space for a personal history):

DATE & TIME	A	B	C	BACKGROUND

The Procedure

The first stage in the management of wandering will help identify whether a consistent pattern exists. In order to get a clear picture, the behaviour should be monitored over a period of weeks in order to avoid making decisions on the basis of short-term fluctuations in behaviour. The information obtained should be shared with all staff, discussed during staff meetings and mentioned at 'handover' reports.

Following the period of observation an accurate interpretation is essential because the information gathered during the behavioural analysis decides which method of solving the problem is most appropriate to the person and their situation.

Misinterpreting the Problem

However, before moving on to the stage of intervention, a word of warning. Whilst in most instances wandering is the result of an interaction between the environment and the elderly person's memory impairment, in a few cases the behaviour may also be the result of localised brain damage. For example, a condition known as visual agnosia (ie an inability to recognise objects by vision alone), can result in sufferers being unable to recognise their carers even in cases where they are close relatives. This may result in feelings of separation anxiety and the onset of wandering. Similarly, it can result in an inability to recognise the 'geography' of a residential home, leading to 'disoriented wandering'. The existence of such a biological change in the brain is bound to seriously interfere with efforts to manage the problem if not taken into consideration. Therefore, assessment of the elderly person by a neuropsychologist should ideally be included in a thorough behavioural analysis, in order to establish the extent of memory loss and whether the presence of other neuropsychological deficits is contributing to the problem. This would avoid the risk of misinterpreting the nature of the wandering behaviour. However, as the expertise to undertake a complete neuropsychological assessment is not readily available, an alternative option is to be aware of the potential existence of unusual neuropsychological deficits. If close observation of the wanderer's behaviour suggests that it is not the result of memory loss but may involve other forms of brain damage (eg recognition problems), then request the involvement of a specialist.

Clearly, whilst seeking an explanation can be a lengthy process, taking the trouble to understand a person's behaviour can save valuable time later. Intervening too quickly with inadequate information about the person and their problem may not only be unhelpful, but is likely to result in the problem assuming crisis proportions.

Keyword Summary

Seeking a detailed explanation
- ABC analysis of behaviour
- When and where did the wandering start?
- What was the person doing before wandering?
- What form did the wandering take?
- What was the response of carers?
- Background information
- Life history – involve the family
- Recording the information
- Finding a pattern – the procedure
- The risk of misinterpretation – the possible existence of focal brain damage
- Neuropsychological assessment
- Saving time in the long run

Management

Safety and Security

It is often the case when confronted with a distressing and seemingly impossible problem that common sense measures are neglected. However, in this section on management, the starting point is the provision of sensible security precautions. This is not to suggest that the use of restraint and confinement is being recommended. The aim of safety and security is to help reduce unnecessary risk and allow carers to be confident that a crisis is less likely to develop through an elderly person unknowingly wandering away and getting lost.

Personal Information

If an elderly person has a tendency to wander it is important that they carry information as to their identity. Such a precaution will aid a speedy return home following their 'apprehension'. However, it is important that the information is carried in a way which does not 'signpost' the elderly person as a wanderer at risk. In all cases involvement with the confused aged must serve to maintain dignity and avoid stigma. The information can be on a tag in a pocket, or placed in a wallet or purse, or even on a label which can be stitched inside their jacket or overcoat. For an elderly woman who wanders the use of an identity bracelet or necklace as a piece of jewellery is a good, albeit more expensive idea and a precaution which would be especially useful for someone who might wander after dark in her night clothes. The information required is:

- Name
- Address
- Telephone number

Providing the confused wanderer with this information not only increases the chances of a safe return home, but it can also act as a memory aid for the elderly person.

The Building

Alarms

Alarms are especially useful when there is a lack of staff for surveillance. They can be installed at the main entrance and other high risk exits to alert nursing and care staff when a resident wanders off the ward or out of the building. The alarms are triggered by a small tag fitted into the clothing of the wanderer. The system is simple to operate and manage.

Any alarm should be unobtrusive so the use of a warning light in the office is a good idea. We are not talking about sirens or deafening alarm bells! It is also important that the staff who are summoned should not create, or add to the confusion of the resident. To avoid unnecessary commotion it may be helpful to nominate a member of staff on each shift to take responsibility for responding to the alarm.

The advantage of an alarm system is that it not only reduces the risk of wanderers getting lost outside or being at risk on the roads, but it also allows doors to be left unlocked thereby allowing the elderly not at risk to be free to come and go as they please.

Locks

Whilst the locking of doors is not to be encouraged in hospitals or residential settings, if the confused wanderer lives at home the security of the front door is an important concern. If a carer is to be allowed to live a life which is as normal as possible – and this means being free of the need to mount a constant watch, being able to go out and leave their confused loved one alone and having a sound night's sleep without worrying about whether their partner has slipped out of the house under the cover of darkness – securing the front door is an essential measure.

The confused elderly have difficulty in re-membering fresh information and learning new ways, and so a new lock on the front door can be a significant barrier to wandering. The more complex the lock the less likely the wanderer is to solve the problem.

As an alternative to a lock which is difficult to operate, locks can also be placed in unfamiliar positions such as at the top and bottom of the front door, thereby making the opening of the door a complicated task.

In institutional settings a way of preventing wandering is to fix handles to the door which need to be pulled simultaneously in opposite directions – a safety measure often used in hospitals. In addition to exits, such a barrier to wandering can be used to protect any area which, if the wanderer were to gain access to, could place them in danger or be an extreme nuisance to staff (eg offices, clinical areas, interview rooms, etc).

Wandering should only be seen as a management problem if it causes danger, inconvenience or disruption. The use of difficult-to-operate handles helps to 'design-out' these unwanted consequences and thereby provides maximum opportunity for physical activity without jeopardising safety. However, it is vital that the elderly wanderer is not deprived of stimulation and interest. Although many wanderers appear content if they are allowed to keep on the move staff should not take this as reason to ignore their quality of life simply because they no longer present as a cause for concern.

It is equally important to avoid a sense of confinement. If a patient is trying to leave the safe area, a complicated arrangement of door handles provides staff with the opportunity to monitor the wanderer's movements or accompany them on their 'journey'. The system is designed to prevent unnoticed disappearances of those confused elderly who are at risk, not a means to enforce protective custody!

Why not look at the building in which the wanderer you are concerned about lives, and see where safety and security could be improved? Ask yourself where the greatest hazards and dangers lie, and remember that the sensible approach to security is to reduce the risk of wandering occurring without introducing major restrictions on the elderly person's activity.

Keyword Summary

- Common sense measures
- Personal information – a discrete precaution
- The building – unobtrusive alarms
- Locks and doors
- The quality of life in 'protected' areas
- **NOT** protective custody

Changing the Environment

Since an elderly person's surroundings play a large part in wandering it makes sense to create an environment that will reduce the risk of this problem arising.

Building Familiarisation

To reduce the likelihood of a person wandering because they cannot locate a specific route or room, the use of signs, symbols and directional arrows can be very effective in making the building more familiar. Signs need to be placed in prominent positions and should be large enough to compensate for poor eyesight. Use simple messages – large pictorial signs or symbols are often better than just the written word. Personalise bedroom doors with the resident's name.

In addition to these 'clues', colour coding may also be helpful. By associating colours with different rooms residents have an alternative key to the geography of the home.

You can imaginatively combine both colour coding and the use of symbols to produce, for example, the following results:

Room	Door	Directional Arrow	Symbol
Toilet	Blue	Blue	Blue 'T' on a white background
Bathroom	White	White	White 'bath' on a blue background
Dining Room	Yellow	Yellow	Yellow 'knife and fork' on a black background
Coffee Room	Brown	Brown	Brown 'cup and saucer' on a yellow background
Bedroom	Orange	Orange	Orange 'bed' on a black background

There are numerous colour combinations, so you can make your choices blend in with the existing decorations and colour scheme. Always remember to use clear lettering and bright colours.

However, it is not enough simply to put up signs and symbols and expect the elderly residents to grasp the meaning. They must also be taught to find their way about. You can introduce the information to a small number of residents in a Reality Orientation group. After this presentation in the 'classroom' staff should accompany confused residents around the home a few times. Eventually, residents should be asked what comes next on the route. Also encourage residents to use their own cues. Get them to notice smells and noises which they can associate with the signs and symbols. This will help them build up a lasting mental map of the home.

Do not walk residents briskly from one location to another. Learning should be at their own pace.

The most confused people will have the greatest difficulty in learning so teaching must take place regularly in order to increase the chances of success.

Be patient, speak slowly and use short simple sentences. If residents make mistakes do not get irritated or critical. If they are successful, show pleasure and approval, but do not be patronising. When this period of orientation is over, give regular reminders about the geography of the home in everyday conversation. Although constant repetition may seem boring to you, it is not to the forgetful and confused.

At Night

With darkness misinterpretations are more likely. What is familiar during the day can appear alien and threatening at night and may result in agitated wandering. A solution is to install night lights in the bedroom and areas the elderly person is likely to want to reach during the night, eg the toilet or bathroom.

The use of a gentle nightlight not only helps reduce disoriented wandering, but it also reduces the likelihood of accidents occurring. Installing a gate at the top of the stairs can also minimise the risk of injury during wandering.

Other changes around the home which can be helpful include hanging curtains made of thick material to block out street light and thereby encourage sleep, making sure the bed is comfortable and the room is neither too hot or too cold and keeping noise and disruptive routines to a minimum. If finding the toilet is particularly troublesome, as a last resort a commode can be provided by the bedside. In a case where fear of being in the bedroom appears to be the reason for a person's insomnia let them sleep in a comfortable chair in the lounge.

As you can see, changing the environment can prevent wandering occurring and can reduce the numerous potential dangers care staff worry about. Clearly it is a valuable option for working with the various types of wandering behaviour.

Keyword Summary

Finding the way
- Signs and directional arrows
- Colour coding
- Learning the geography of a home
- Effective teaching techniques
- Regular reminders

At night
- The benefits of nightlights
- Encouraging sleep – restructuring the surroundings

⟨7⟩

Behavioural Methods

Behavioural management has shown itself to be a powerful means of modifying problem behaviour. A decision to use this method arises, for example, when following a behavioural analysis it is decided that changing the consequences of wandering may lead to a reduction in frequency of occurrence.

Behaviour Modification

In general, the basic idea is, when it is safe to do so, to deny wanderers fuss and attention whilst they are roaming about. Instead, you reward them with your time and approval only at such times as they are doing something which is incompatible with wandering, such as sitting quietly or participating in a constructive behaviour. This practice not only dissuades attention-seekers from wandering, but also serves to improve the quality of people's lives by encouraging them to join in the activities of the home.

When giving praise, be sure that you do not treat the elderly person as a child or appear in any way condescending. To do so may not only serve to annoy, but could easily undermine confidence and remind elderly people of their failing powers. When communicating with an elderly person, the aim must always be to maintain their self-respect.

However, this method of control will only work if what is given as a reward is seen by the wanderer as rewarding and pleasurable. It is *not* the opinion of the carer which matters. Whilst the approval and attention of a carer may sometimes be a reward in itself, it is not always enough. In this case, you will have to enrich the life of the wanderer by providing them with small tangible rewards which they can either use or consume. Another option is to provide the opportunity for exercise and outings as a reward.

If you are able to persuade an elderly person to stop wandering, the reward should be given immediately; otherwise, if there is a delay, they may not remember why they are being rewarded and thus wandering may continue.

Learning to Discriminate

A more sophisticated behavioural approach is to teach a resident when wandering is acceptable and when it is not. This involves the use of large symbols of two different designs, each approximately eighteen inches in diameter. The first design, for example, yellow arrows, would be paired with a reward. These would be strategically placed along a route within the home avoiding hazardous points and leading the wanderer to safe areas, such as the lounge or garden. These symbols need to be prominent and colourful so that they are easily noticed by the habitual wanderer. The other design, say a red triangle, would be located at danger points, such as the main entrance, fire exits and stairs. This design would be paired with a mildly unpleasant experience, such as a loud hand-clap. Alternatively, the wanderer would always be escorted away from these locations and re-directed toward the safe route where wandering would not be discouraged. In this way a wanderer would learn, when faced with a particular symbol, whether his wandering would be prevented or allowed to continue.

Rather than solely using a hazard-warning symbol, colour-coding can once again be used to deter wanderers from entering high-risk areas. For example, the areas and doors could be coloured red with a symbol of a red lightening flash on a white background.

Information on the reason for the symbols and their consequences can be given in reality orientation sessions. After an initial training period, booster-training sessions would be required at regular intervals to make sure the colours and symbols retained their meaning for the wanderer. Once the system has been soundly grasped the cues can be gradually reduced in size.

Evidence shows that when this behavioural method has been used there has been a reduction in the number of times wandering occurred in dangerous areas; it also enables active wanderers to safely continue their habit elsewhere.

General Principles

Overall, it is essential that behavioural management operates as far as is possible twenty-four hours a day, seven days a week, especially with the more severely confused elderly. All care staff must be involved in order to guarantee that the resident is treated consistently, for consistency is one of the most important features of this approach.

Finally, and possibly most importantly, before you embark upon behavioural management you must be confident that the elderly confused person will be able to benefit from the procedures. In other words, the target being planned for the resident must be realistic and attainable. The problem of memory loss should not be so severe that the goal will always remain incomprehensible and perplexing. To ensure that this does not happen, keep a record of performance and ensure that all carers review progress regularly.

Keyword Summary

Behaviour modification
- Changing the consequences of wandering
- When to give attention
- Reward constructive behaviour
- Maintain self-respect and dignity
- Find rewards that please
- Reward immediately

A learning situation
- Hazard warning system – the use of symbols
- Discuss in reality orientation groups
- Booster-training sessions

General principles
- The need for a consistent approach
- Set realistic targets
- Record-keeping and regular reviews

8

Activity and Exercise

The need for interest, exercise and companionship may be responsible for much of the wandering observed in residential homes and long-stay hospital units. So rather than seeking ways to manage the problem while it is occurring, another approach is to increase the amount of activity available during the day with the aim of preventing it happening in the first place.

Activities

When it comes to providing interesting activities, we should not assume that all elderly residents enjoy 'arts and crafts' or bingo. Find out what their previous work roles and hobbies were and aim to provide activities they are more likely to enjoy. This may involve not only traditional occupational activities, but also small jobs and tasks around the home. Making the signs and symbols described in earlier chapters can be a useful occupation. Reminiscence sessions are often popular. For both individuals and groups, outings and shopping expeditions are enjoyable, providing they are not arduous and do not involve much travelling. Even though the confused may not appreciate where they are, they will enjoy a change of scenery. Overall, the provision of interesting things to do is likely to reduce boredom and prevent day-time catnapping.

Sociability

In addition to compensating for the loss of activity in the life of a confused resident, feelings of loneliness and rejection need to be dealt with too. If you cannot get family or friends to visit, try arranging for a volunteer helper to visit and 'adopt' the old person.

To encourage friendships between residents try to involve them in regular social activities. Keep group membership constant so that faces become familiar.

It is also important to consider the seating arrangements in the day room or lounge. Social contact between residents is often discouraged by the arrangement of chairs, which are normally situated around the walls of the room and thus reduce opportunity to talk as most residents have either to shout to each other across the room or strain to turn round to face their neighbour. It is a far better idea to arrange the chairs around coffee-tables as this encourages conversation. The tables can then also be used for small group activities.

Care staff should not equate talking to residents or patients with wasting time, nor should they feel guilty about doing so. Whilst carers invariably talk to residents as they are doing things for them, the conversation is normally mechanical and often dominated by the task at hand. Not surprisingly, this kind of interaction does little to reduce loneliness. So try not to be too busy to talk with the elderly in your care. In many ways it is the responsibility of senior staff to ensure that junior nurses and care assistants understand that spending time with the elderly is an essential part of the job.

Exercise

Some wanderers appear to be on self-assigned exercise programmes. These may be people who have led very active lives or had physically demanding jobs. For such habitual wanderers, who have seemingly limitless energy, the scheduling of physical activity will help satisfy the need for exercise. Walks outside in the fresh air are ideal, so if there is a garden available, make full use of it. Residents who have structured periods of exercise during the day are more likely to sleep at night. Whilst the exercise should not be strenuous, it is wise to check whether the old person is fit enough to join in.

Once these stimulation and exercise programmes are introduced, they should remain a lasting feature of the home, for the benefits which are to be gained would not be maintained if the activities were to stop. Therefore care staff need to have plenty of enthusiasm and ingenuity to keep the residents interested and keen to participate in the social and recreational life of the home.

Keyword Summary

Activity
- Finding activities which are enjoyable
- Small jobs around the home
- Outings

Sociability
- Encouraging visitors
- Social activities
- Seating arrangements in the day room
- Talking to residents/patients is part of the job

Exercise
- Physical activity
- Walks outside
- Are the elderly fit enough to participate?

Maintaining the social and recreational life of the home

Psychological Methods

There are specific psychological methods that can be used to help ease the management strain of caring for a wanderer.

Reality Orientation

During times of disorientation and confusion reality testing is of great importance. Be sure you are in possession of accurate information. Remind the wanderer of the time, where they are and who you are. Explain all that is strange and do not take anything for granted. Always correctly identify the wanderer. Whatever form of address is chosen it should always be used consistently and respectfully.

The wanderer is likely to be bothered and agitated, so be friendly, patient and understanding. To reduce anxiety levels, reassure wanderers that their worries are groundless. However, remember that you also have the task of trying to make the confused aware of their surroundings. For example:

Time orientation: "Mrs Simpson, it is one o'clock in the morning. See how dark it is."

Place orientation: "This is Greenpark Lodge, Mrs Jones. This is where you live. See the sign on the wall."

Person orientation: "Mrs Green, my name is Sue. I work on this ward. Do you want me to call you Elsie or Mrs Green?"

At night quietly talk to those who cannot sleep and reassure them about their whereabouts. If they have already started to wander often all that is needed is a gentle reminder that it is still night-time, and then to lead them back to bed. However, you are likely to be at your lowest ebb if you have been awakened, possibly feeling tired and irritable, so remember to be tolerant and speak softly and gently.

The most effective way to correct inaccurate and rambling speech is to help the confused realise that their beliefs are mistaken and inappropriate. Be logical and rational. Help them discover the existence of errors by asking *them* to test reality. Do their statements coincide with the evidence? Your approach must always be non-threatening, always ultimately providing the correct information. However, remember this is reality orientation *not* reality confrontation, so do not argue. If the wanderer cannot be persuaded it is unwise to persist with your efforts.

Finally, the confused with sensory handicaps have an even greater need for reality orientation. If the problems of damaged hearing and poor eyesight cannot be corrected, compensate for the sensory losses by helping the confused identify reality through the use of all five senses: taste, smell, touch, hearing and vision.

Distraction

There is always a need to avoid mishandling a wanderer. As it is never advisable to risk a confrontation, how do you approach an elderly person who is wandering and encourage them to do otherwise?

An effective method is to distract them. Rather than directly confronting them, try talking about something other than what is going on. Approach them calmly and speak in short simple sentences. While respecting the elderly person's need for personal space in order to feel comfortable, a gentle and reassuring touch on the hand or arm can aid communication. Your aim is to get them to forget their intention to wander and divert them to another activity. If you know your resident well, you should be able to talk about a topic that gains their attention. Talking about the past can effectively occupy the mind of a wanderer. If wandering is occurring because of a need to search for somebody or something from long ago, reminiscing as a means of distraction can be especially effective. It is made easier if the old person has kept personal possessions, such as photographs or momentos, which can be the focus of conversation.

Collusion

If the wanderer is not disturbing anybody and is not in immediate danger, but is likely to get lost if not closely monitored, go along with the behaviour. By simply accompanying the wanderer and thereby allowing them to continue, you are colluding.

One technique to help combat the problem of wandering away from a home or ward involves two staff members. One member of staff approaches the wanderer and colludes for several minutes with no attempt to encourage a return, unless the wanderer wishes to do so. Be friendly and casually chat. Eventually the second staff member arrives and asks *both* of them to return with her. If the wanderer does not agree, the first carer says they will return, but in 15 minutes. In this way the likelihood of a confrontation is reduced and trust between the wanderer and care staff is developed. On return to the home or ward it is unwise for any member of staff to show annoyance or irritation because this will be seen as a sign of punishment and will discourage the resident from returning if wandering should re-occur.

By giving you guidelines on how to communicate with a perhaps determined and muddled wanderer, these psychological techniques can help you avoid a potentially catastrophic confrontation.

Keyword Summary

Reality orientation

- Reality testing
- Be friendly, patient and understanding
- Time, place and person orientation
- Be logical and rational
- It is *not* reality *con*frontation
- Helping those with sensory handicaps

Distraction

- Talk about something else
- A calm approach
- The value of touch
- Reminiscing

Collusion

- Going along with the behaviour
- A practical technique to control wandering
- Developing trust between wanderer and care staff

The Supporters

Helpful Attitudes

Be Positive

Positive staff attitudes are the key to the success of most of the ideas discussed in this book. It does not matter how effective these methods appear in theory, if the attitudes of those who are putting them into practice are unhelpful, they are doomed to fail.

Without being too optimistic, expect improvement. It can occur; deterioration is not inevitable. If success is not achieved with one approach, try another way. Time and time again we have seen the behaviour of the elderly confused improve when thoughtful management is introduced, yet many carers continue to act as if this were impossible.

So, try not to be rigid in your beliefs, and if necessary, re-adjust your attitudes and expectations.

The Whole Person

Do not simply look upon the wanderer as a problem to be removed. Instead consider the whole person. The wanderer exhibits unwanted behaviour, but include this in an appreciation of the person as an individual with a colourful history and a wealth of achievements – a person who has needs, feelings, likes and dislikes.

While confusion may be a barrier to communication and thus make it difficult to appreciate how experiences have shaped an elderly person's life, an interest in the whole individual helps us to better understand the aged wanderer and this must inevitably lead to an improvement in the quality of care provided.

The Problem in Perspective

Do not over-react or feel overwhelmed by having to be responsible for a wanderer.

Action does not have to be taken. If no harm is being done and the wanderer is not at risk, ask yourself whether you need to do anything at all. Wandering may be unattractive, but is it unacceptable? Sometimes it is best to leave the behaviour alone and accept the situation.

Burn-out

When many confused elderly are gathered together problems can appear insurmountable. To manage one wanderer may be difficult, to care for several can appear impossible.

You may approach your work with enthusiasm, yet soon become dismayed and discouraged by the physical demands, unsocial hours and inadequate support.

In these situations you need to share your

anger, disappointment and grievances. If you do not, you risk experiencing "burnout" – feelings of frustration, exhaustion, demoralisation and hopelessness. So, as a regular practice, seek the mutual support of colleagues. Hold group meetings to exchange experiences and concerns. Do not feel embarrassed to acknowledge your doubts and weaknesses, for you will also undoubtedly have assets and strengths your fellow carers may benefit from.

However, if you work in relative isolation and there is little chance of assistance from other carers, try and develop coping attitudes. Dismiss negative and self-defeating ideas. Do not let your mind run riot to the extent where you "cannot see the wood for the trees". Be constructive and concentrate on the task in hand. The demands and pressures may appear endless but you will only successfully get on top of them if you tackle one problem at a time. Positive thinking can help prevent undesirable levels of stress and strain.

Overall, adopting the right attitudes can not only help the elderly confused obtain a better quality of life, but can make you a more effective carer.

Attitudes

- Be positive
- Remain confident that improvement will occur

The whole person

- Treat the wanderer as a person, not simply as a problem
- Take an interest in the whole person – appreciate needs and feelings

The problem in perspective

- Do not over-react
- Is the behaviour unacceptable?

Burn-out

- Problems appear insurmountable
- Enthusiasm replaced by dismay
- Burn-out – feelings of exhaustion and frustration
- The need for the support of colleagues
- Coping attitudes – dismiss negative ideas
- Be constructive – tackle one problem at a time

Being the 'Therapist'

Not Just a Carer

As we have seen, the effective management of wandering is not something that can be switched on and off. It needs to be practised day in, day out. Such a demand for '24-hour therapy' inevitably involves nurses and residential workers.

The routine work of care staff in daily contact and communication with the elderly wanderer means they have a major impact on management. Only those working so closely with the problem can identify the most likely explanations and possible solutions. The more familiar you and your colleagues are with the elderly person, the more accurate your knowledge will be. Nobody else can possibly be so well informed. No other professional can appreciate the difficulties that arise from day-to-day. In practice you therefore cease to be simply a carer and become a skilled 'therapist' in your own right.

Medication

Hand-in-hand with an increase in the 'therapeutic' role of carers is the view that the management of wandering residents or patients does not inevitably require the use of sedating drugs. Do not rely on medication to solve the problem. Whilst sedation may reduce the frequency of wandering, because of the possibility of side- and after-effects it should be used very sparingly and only as a last resort. For example, the careful administration of prescribed night sedation can encourage sleep. However, if used unwisely it can result in drowsiness and heightened confusion the next day.

Overall, medication is an inadequate substitute for patience, understanding and a regime which satisfies the needs of the elderly confused in care.

Strategy

The guidelines for all therapeutic supporters should be to:

• Identify the reason for wandering.
• Make a plan to manage it.
• Put the plan into action.
• Evaluate the extent to which the plan is effective.

Such an approach is likely not only to reduce the burden of responsibility but also to improve your own skills and increase the satisfaction you get from your job.

Keyword Summary

More than a carer

- Good management practice cannot be switched on and off
- 24-hour therapy
- Effective management requires accurate information
- Nurses and care-staff are the best informed
- Being a skilled 'therapist'

Medication

- Do not rely on sedating medication
- Possible side- and after-effects
- Drugs – a poor substitute for patience and understanding

Therapeutic strategy

- Find the cause
- Design a treatment plan
- Put plan into operation
- Evaluate the outcome

12

Managing the Problem at Home

There are around 500,000 confused elderly people, yet less than a quarter of them are cared for in hospitals or residential homes. The family is, without any doubt, the main provider of care. Typically, the responsibility of care lies with a partner, daughter or daughter-in-law. Yet relatives struggling to cope with behaviour often as difficult as that found in institutional settings are frequently the forgotten sufferers.

Although nobody outside the situation really knows what it is like to live with a person who wanders, it is hoped that some of the ideas described in this book will make the task of caring easier. To end this practical guide here are a few more points to help relatives cope with their unenviable situation.

The Future

Wandering does not commonly worsen over time. Nor does wandering entail the appearance of other disruptive behaviours. So you may look to the future with a degree of optimism, for if you are managing to cope with your loved one's tendency to wander at present, there is a good chance that you will continue to do so.

Coping with Feelings

It is common to have negative and upsetting feelings when caring for someone who regularly wanders. Do not be ashamed of these.

Wandering can make you so concerned about possible dangers that you become over-anxious and over-protective. This can make you feel that you are never free of the problem, so try and place limits on your sense of duty. This is made easier if you have a true appreciation of the possible hazards and risks.

It is understandable to grieve for the loss of companionship as major personality changes occur in those you love.

As persistent wandering is extremely taxing for the carer, so anger is a common and natural response. However, try to be angry with the behaviour and not the person. You may also be angry with fate at having been so unkind. You may also be resentful with other members of the family who are not 'pulling their weight'. If you are unable to contain your discontent, you obviously need to do something. Share your feelings and demand support or relief.

Some carers become so enmeshed in their situation that life can appear a never-ending round of supervision and responsibility. It can help if you try to emotionally distance yourself from your problem. When you feel stressed and anxious check whether your worries are largely unfounded or exaggerated. Abandon "what if . . ." thoughts. Ask yourself whether there is any evidence to support your fears. Reduce the pressure you feel by avoiding such ideas as "I shouldn't be doing this" or "I must do that"; such thoughts increase the demands you place on yourself and make caring even more tiring.

Wandering is difficult enough to handle without your inflicting more and more pressure upon yourself.

Some carers benefit from placing not only an emotional distance between themselves and their caring responsibilities, but also, on occasions, a physical distance. Whenever possible get out, do things, meet people and generally have a break from what may be an upsetting and demanding routine.

Resources

Do not be reluctant to seek professional help. Contact your GP or local Social Services office to request practical support. The Citizens Advice Bureau may have useful tips about local services and facilities. If you want information about the nature of the problem you are dealing with, there are voluntary organisations such as the Alzheimer's Disease Society which are able to provide expert guidance. Often receiving an explanation provides immense relief.

To provide good care you must consider your own needs. Increasing the resources available to you can reduce the cost of caring and ensure that you are able to continue in your supporting role. Encourage other family members to help you share out the responsibility. Do any relatives live close at hand? Could they occasionally come over and keep a watchful eye while you have a day or evening out?

Finally, never feel guilty about no longer being able to be the sole care giver, or your inability to manage without help. These are irrational and self-destructive beliefs. Nobody expects you to be either superhuman or a martyr.

Practical Suggestions

If you are embarrassed by a relative who keeps wandering from the house, visit neighbours and explain the reason for the behaviour. This course of action may result in increased tolerance and understanding, or even in your neighbours being more willing to keep an eye on the wanderer's movements.

In the home, as in a residential setting, prevention of wandering is a better management strategy than trying to think of ways of coping with the problem while it is taking place. So always bear in mind that simple, predictable and familiar routines help reduce the likelihood of confused behaviour.

Work at trying to improve your loved one's memory. This can be aided by having a place for everything and putting everything in its place. Make sure there is easy access to everyday information. For example, put up a 'memory board' in the kitchen or another prominent place. Make sure you include information on the day's activities and especially details of your movements and whereabouts. This is essential if you plan to go out as it will help reduce feelings of separation anxiety. When left alone, always leave your loved one with something to do to occupy their mind.

If the wanderer wears a watch, make sure it is accurate. If they are fit and able, encourage them to do chores around the house. This will not only give them interest but will also reduce their dependence upon you. If confidence can be gained from being involved in the domestic routine wanderers are less likely to feel vulnerable should you need to leave them alone.

Whilst it is advisable to make your absence from home predictable so that it becomes part of a regular pattern, this is not always possible. Always leave a note explaining where you are and when you will return. An alternative is to leave a tape-recorded (or even a videotaped) message giving factual and reassuring information. This is obviously a more comforting reminder. To overcome the problem of the wanderer forgetting a taped message has been left, intense training will have to take place for them to recall when and how to switch on the machine. Looking to the future, it should not be beyond the ingenuity of the manufacturers of clinical aids to develop a technology by which the recording could play automatically when the agitated wanderer steps on a pressure pad located, for example, by the door. The equipment could then be made available from GPs or Social Services. Given that so many carers feel trapped by their loved one's handicap this would be a worthwhile challenge and development.

Although wandering can make life particularly difficult for supporting relatives, always remain confident that improvement can occur. Use the information in this book to open your mind to ideas and practical suggestions which you may never have considered. It may enable you to make the best of what must often seem an impossible situation.

Keyword Summary

The forgotten suffers
- The family is the main provider of care

The Future
- Wandering – deterioration is not inevitable
- Wandering does not necessarily lead to other disruptive behaviours
- Be optimistic

Coping
- Do not be ashamed of your feelings
- Over-anxious and over-protective
- Anger is a natural reaction – be angry at the behaviour
- Share your feelings
- Emotional distance can be helpful
- Abandon 'what if' thoughts
- Watch out for the pressure words – I *must*, I *should*, etc
- Take a break

Resources
- Seek professional help
- Citizens Advice Bureax may have useful information
- Recruit family members to help out
- Needing help – do not feel guilty
- Do not be a martyr

Practical suggestions

- Involve neighbours
- Simple and predictable routines are helpful
- A place for everything, and everything in its place
- Memory board
- Clocks and watches – are they accurate?
- Promote independence
- Going out
  - provide occupation
  - make absences from home predictable
  - leave a message
  - future technology

---◇---

Appendix I
Useful Organisations

Alzheimer's Disease Society, 3rd Floor, Bank Buildings, Fulham Broadway, London SW6 1EP

Age Concern England, Bernard Sunley House, Pitcairn Road, Mitcham, Surrey CR4 3LL

Age Concern Scotland, 33 Castle Street, Edinburgh EH2 3DN

Age Concern Wales, 1 Park Grove, Cardiff CF1 3B

Association of Carers, Medway Homes, Balfour Road, Rochester, Kent ME4 6QU

Coventry Association for the Carers of the Elderly Confused, Newfield Lodge Day Centre, Kingfield Road, Coventry CV1 4DW

Disabled Living Foundation, 346 Kensington High Street, London W14 8NS

Help the Aged, 16-18 St James Walk, London EC1R 0BE

National Council for Carers and their Elderly Dependants, 29 Chilworth Mews, London W2 3RG

—— ◇ ——

Appendix II
Further Reading for Carers

Forgetfulness in Elderly Persons, Advice for Carers, Age Concern.

Coping with Caring — A Guide to Identifying and Supporting an Elderly Person with Dementia, Brian Lodge, MIND, 1981.

24-Hour Approach to the Problem of Confusion in Elderly People, Una Holden et al, Winslow Press, London, 1980.

Our Elders, G.K. Wilcock & J.A. Muir Gray, Oxford University Press, 1981.

Coping with Ageing Parents, C.J. Gilleard & G. Watt, MacDonald Ltd., Loanhead, Midlothian, 1983.

Thinking It Through, U. Holden, Winslow Press, London, 1984.

Caring for the Person with Dementia, Alzheimer's Disease Society, 1984.

Living with Dementia, C.J. Gilleard, Croom Helm Ltd., Beckenham, Kent, 1984.

The 36-Hour Day, N.L. Mace & P.V. Rabins, Hodder & Stoughton, London, 1985.